Dear Professor, Do You Live in a Vacuum?

For Kassapa~

All-My best,

Nm Andrews

Nin Andrews

Dear Professor,
Do You Live in a Vacuum?

Subito Press / Boulder, Colorado / 2008

Subito Press
Boulder, Colorado
www.subitopress.org

Printed in the United States of America

Several of the *Dear Professor, Do You Live in a Vacuum?*
poems have appeared in *TriQuarterly Review* and are
forthcoming in the anthology *Brady's Leap*.

Library of Congress Cataloging-in-Publication Data
available upon request.

ISBN 978-0-9801098-2-5

Generous funding for this publication has been pro-
vided by the Creative Writing Program in the Depart-
ment of English at the University of Colorado, Boulder,
as well as the United Government of Graduate Stu-
dents (UGGS).

*For my husband, Jim, and his students over the years
whose comments, e-mails, notes, and questions
inspired many of the poems in this collection.*

Dear Professor,

I hope you don't mind that I e-mail you
and leave notes.
I keep journals full of questions,
and I love to ask for help.
It's the way I learn.
I could phone you too,
but I stay up late at night,
and I noticed your phone number is unlisted.

Dear Professor,

When I told Dr. Z, my religion professor,
that I was actually taking physics,
he was surprised. *Really?*
he asked. Then he admitted
he didn't know much about physics.
I figure that's okay.
I'm pretty sure you don't know much about God.

.

Dear Professor,

I asked Joe, the TA, what the answer was
to problems 3 and 4,
and he said it might help
if I went home and thought about it
for an evening.
"Just thinking about it"
has never helped solved
any of my problems.

Dear Professor,

I read this article about the difference
between men and women
and why men are good at math and science
and women are good with people.
It said men have monotracking brains.
They can focus on one thing
and only one thing at a time.
When men brush their teeth, for example,
they stand with their feet a foot apart,
their heads bent over the sink
concentrating.
This relates to how they solve math problems.
I did notice that Joe has really clean teeth.

Dear Professor,

When I was in your office
and you showed me that problem
about the weight lifter and the dumbbells,
I kept smiling and saying yes,
but I didn't really understand a word you were saying.
I tried, but it's like you were speaking
a different language.
I think new professors do that.
They get lost in translation.
So I thought maybe I should tell you
that when a student smiles and nods and says yes
a lot,
what she really means is she has no idea
what you're talking about.

Dear Professor,

I still don't believe heavy
and light things fall at the same speed.
A feather and a stone, for example.
You kept saying I'd get it
if I lived in a vacuum.
Do you live in a vacuum?

Dear Professor,

I am glad that you said
physics and math are not the same.
The specific numbers or right answers
are the least important factors in my equations.
Right answers have never been my thing.

Dear Professor,

I started my homework last night,
and I couldn't do problem 1.
I wasn't sure about 2 either.
I wrote a few things down,
but I thought I'd come by your office
and see if you could help me
with the rest of the problems.
Would that be a problem?

Dear Professor,

Joe had a flat tire this morning.
At first Joe said he thought the car was leaning
to one side because I was getting so fat.
I could have come to class at half past,
but I wanted to show you the courtesy
of not interrupting your class.
And I wanted to punch Joe.
I thought I'd write you, though,
just to be sure you knew
why I wasn't there.
It wasn't your fault.
I wouldn't want you to take it personally.

Dear Professor,

Don't ask me any questions.
Or expect me to raise my hand.
I'm listening.
I just don't want anyone to know
if I get the wrong answer.
I'm sitting here.
That should be participation enough.

Dear Professor,

I was in line at your office during your office hours,
and one student kept talking and talking.
I thought she'd never stop.
I think you should do us all a favor
and limit her to one question,
then make her go back to the end of the line.
Otherwise, once we get our turns,
we'll never leave either.
And you'll never get anything done.

Dear Professor,

I went to Barnes & Noble
to purchase *Physics for Dummies*
or the *Idiot's Guide to Physics*.
But those books didn't help me at all.
The authors of those books
have no idea how a dummy thinks.

Dear Professor,

I think it's very unfair that you ask me questions
about accelerating in a car.
I am not like those students
who drive to school in their nice cars.
I don't even know how to drive,
and I don't expect to be learning any time soon.

Dear Professor,

I had to work late at Steak 'n Shake.
I got home and was so burnt out
I had a few beers and before I knew it,
I fell asleep. I came to class
hung over. I just thought you might
want to know what happened to me,
in case you were wondering
why my head kept jerking up and down
like that. I'm not epileptic or anything.

Dear Professor,

You keep saying that science
is all about proof.
If you prove that what we believe is wrong,
we should change our minds.
But minds don't change like that.
We keep proving it
every time we take another test.

Dear Professor,

I heard you complaining
about our class.
A huge class, you said.
No one is learning a darn thing.
Consider Newton's
2nd and 3rd laws.
We have a lot of mass.
The more you push us,
the more we push right back.

Dear Professor,

I think if I were a guy,
I'd have a better chance of answering
the questions about the impact
of a bat on a ball.
Have you ever considered that men
and women have anatomical differences?
That our physics might not be
the same thing as yours?

Dear Professor,

I think I screwed up the midterm.
Please talk to me before you grade it.
I can tell you what I know.
I studied really hard, and I learned a lot,
and that's not on the test.

Dear Professor,

My coach said to write you,
'cause I'll miss five Friday classes.
I'll miss one Wednesday class
if we make it to Regionals,
and I'll have to postpone my exams.
I'll meet you for office hours and do make-ups.
I promise. Also I have a job,
and I work on Monday mornings
so I will be late to class on Mondays,
because my boss says he can't always
make his schedule around me.

Dear Professor,

I hate it when I'm in class,
and you use all those technical terms
like kinematics and mass and velocity
and stuff. I always feel like
you're a walking textbook.
I want to ask you one day
if you can put something in your own words.

Dear Professor,

You keep running around the classroom,
monitoring our experiments,
and checking our work,
hoping we'll get it . . .
Like maybe we'll have some kind of
eureka moment.
Do we look like Archimedes in the bathtub?

Dear Professor,

Dr. Z says physics can't explain everything,
because there are always ways
around the laws of physics.
For example, certain monks can walk through fire
and not burn.
He licked his finger and waved it
right through a flame
to prove his point.

Dear Professor,

Today you said if X is in such-and-such a position
when X's momentum is so-and-so
or such-and-such,
then we should be able to solve
for if-and-when,
because so-and-so times such-and-such is if-and-when.
I just have to tell you,
this is what I hate about science.
Like where's the mystery in that?

Dear Professor,

Dr. Z said he put his microwave oven out on the curb.
He read that microwaves are dangerous.
They can get out of the ovens.
You can't feel them,
but you've seen
what they do to a baked potato.

Dear Professor,

You gave that problem
about driving down the freeway at 60 MPH
in a VW bug and hitting a truck
that was driving at 75 MPH,
and you wanted to know what happened next,
and I figured the answer was simple.
Drive a truck from now on.

Dear Professor,

I couldn't answer any questions on page 5 of the test,
so I wrote an essay on $E=Mc^2$.
I love $E=Mc^2$.
I think it's the lynchpin of the universe.
It explains everything
that isn't in your class.

Dear Professor,

I had a hard time on the second part
of the test. I was really tired.
And I had to go to the bathroom,
but I was afraid to go.
I thought you might think
I was cheating in there.

Dear Professor,

My friend in the business school, Tom,
has this really smart idea
for a perpetual motion machine.
It will work too.
He just has to harness gravity.
In order to complete it,
all he needs is to learn a little science.
As soon as he gets his patent,
he wants to talk to you.

Dear Professor,

I just discovered the new universal law
for students like me:
the conservation of confusion.
Confusion, like energy,
is neither created nor destroyed.
It never vanishes.
It merely changes forms.

Dear Professor,

I'm preparing for your exam
in Quantum.
Which means I am waiting
for the nonzero probability
that my brilliance
will manifest on its own.
It's bound to happen.
There's just no telling when.

Dear Professor,

I know you love this stuff,
because you bring in those kits
and little physics "toys."
Like balls of string
and lights and magnets . . .
Yesterday you mentioned some famous scientist
who even dreamt about Buckyballs.
I've been thinking about that guy a lot.
Are Buckyballs the kind of thing
you think of
before going to sleep?

Dear Professor,

I heard the Brian Greene talk
on string theory. He even showed pictures
of these stringy things.
Like vibes. That explains everything.
And I had really good vibes about Brian Greene.
Do you know if he's single?

Dear Professor,

I think Brian Greene HAS to be right.
He says we're all connected
spiritually and stringily.
Now we just have to locate
the strings inside the theory.

Dear Professor,

You asked if I listened in class today.
And I am writing you now
to show you that I did listen.
You said that if the uncertainty of one is zero,
then the uncertainty of the other is infinite.
It's just that you're one,
and I'm the other one.

Dear Professor,

I wasn't late.
As Quantum proves,
I have my own personal clock.
So relative to me and my day
I was right on time.

Dear Professor,

Maybe I'd get physics
if I saw the earth pushing my feet up,
if I watched a man throw a ball,
and the ball threw his arm back,
if I saw feathers and stones falling side by side,
if I saw light moving like ocean waves,
rising, cresting, and falling outside my window,
and if I didn't fear my mind is a black hole
in which all you teach me
vanishes forever.

Dear Professor,

I couldn't take the final,
because I was in jail,
because I was at this high stakes poker game
in inner-city Cleveland over the weekend,
and I got busted,
and my lawyer said not to tell a soul,
because it might jeopardize my case,
so I couldn't call you or anyone
to explain what happened
and why I wasn't there.
But I'm back now,
and I'm ready to take my exam.

Dear Professor,

This is what I've learned in your class:
when in doubt, solve for X,
even if there is no X,
especially if there is no X.

Dear Professor,

Dr. Z is a lot kinder than you with his extra credits.
He said we could improve our grades
as much as 10% by doing extra projects.
I did three so he raised my grade 30%.
You said extra credit was worth 5%,
and I did loads of extra credit problems
and they still only counted for 5% of my grade.
What good is 5%? That's like giving someone
a single sock when she has no clothes.

Dear Professor,

In describing a photon,
you said that a photon is not a wave,
and it's not *not* a wave.
And I'm saying that I'm not with you,
and I'm not *not* with you.

Dear Professor,

I sometimes think
that physics whizzes like you and Joe
don't live in the real world.
You might not even know
what real world means. Like
maybe you live in a hypothetical world.

Dear Professor,

So you say a wave can be in two places
at the same time,
and a particle can't.
And they're the same thing
and not the same thing.
Or there are two ways
that something can appear
to be or not to be.
Now we're getting to where Hamlet
and physics overlap.

Dear Professor,

I should have dropped your class.
If I'd known how badly I was going to do,
I'd have found another way to get credit.
All I needed was a C.
There should be a class for people like me.
It might be a relief for both of us.
Think about it.
You wouldn't expect very much,
and we wouldn't disappoint you.

Dear Professor,

Joe came over last night
when I was reciting this poem by Rilke,
so Joe started reciting
random numbers . . .
He even wrote them down for me
so I could do it too:
3.1415926535
8979323846 . . .
I would like to know:
is this what poetry sounds like to a physicist?

Nin Andrews' poems and stories have appeared in many literary journals and anthologies, including *Ploughshares*, *The Paris Review*, *Best American Poetry (1997, 2001, 2003)*, and *Great American Prose Poems*. She won an individual artist grant from the Ohio Arts Council in 1997 and again in 2003. She is the author of several books, including *Spontaneous Breasts*, winner of the Pearl Chapbook Contest; *Any Kind of Excuse*, winner of the Kent State University chapbook contest; *The Book of Orgasms*, published by Cleveland State University Press; *The Book of Orgasms and Other Tales*, published in England by Bloodaxe Books and currently being translated into Turkish; and *Why They Grow Wings*, published by Silverfish Press and winner of the Gerald Cable Award.

She is also the editor of a book of translations of the French poet Henri Michaux entitled *Someone Wants to Steal My Name*, published by Cleveland State University Press. Her book *Midlife Crisis with Dick and Jane* is newly published from *Web del Sol*. Her book *Sleeping with Houdini* is newly published by BOA Editions. Her book *Southern Comfort* is forthcoming from CavanKerry Press.